Kids' Travel Guide
France

FlyingKids Presents:

Kids' Travel Guide France

Writer: Shira Halperin
Editor: Yael Ornan
Designer: Keren Amram, Slavisa Zivkovic
Cover Designer: Francesca Guido
Illustrator: Liat Aluf
Translator: Oren Amir
Translation editor: Carma Graber

Published by FlyingKids Limited

Visit us: www.theflyingkids.com
Contact us: leonardo@theflyingkids.com

ISBN: 978-1-910994-04-7

Copyright © 2015 Shira Halperin and FlyingKids Limited

All rights reserved. No part of this publication may be reproduced, stored in retrieval systems, or transmitted by any means, including electronic, mechanical, photocopying, or otherwise, without prior written permission of the publisher and copyright holder.

Although the authors and FlyingKids have taken all reasonable care in preparing this book, we make no warranty about the accuracy or completeness of its content and, to the maximum extent permitted, disclaim all liability arising from its use.

Acknowledgment: All images by FlyingKids or public domain, except those mentioned below.
Shutterstock images: pp. 10, 15, 27, 29, 32, 33 & 37; Dollar Photo Club: PP. 11 & 16.

Hi, Kids!

If you are reading this book, it means you are lucky — you are going to **France**!

You may have noticed that your parents are getting ready for the journey. They have bought travel guides, looked for information on the Internet, and printed pages of information. They are talking to friends and people who have already visited France, in order to learn about it and know what to do, where to go, and when...

But this book is not just another guidebook for your parents.
This book is for you only — for the young traveler.

So what is this book all about?

First and foremost, meet **Leonardo**, your very own personal guide on this trip. Leonardo has visited **many places** around the world (guess how he got there? 🙂), and he will be with you throughout the book and the trip until you return home. Leonardo will tell you all about the places you will visit — it is always good to learn a little bit about the country and its history beforehand. He will provide many ideas, quizzes, tips, and **other surprises.** Leonardo will accompany you while you are packing and leaving home. He will stay in the hotel with you (don't worry, it does not cost more money 😉)! And he will visit the **sites** with you until you return home and paste your pictures on the right pages, turning this into a wonderful book of memories.

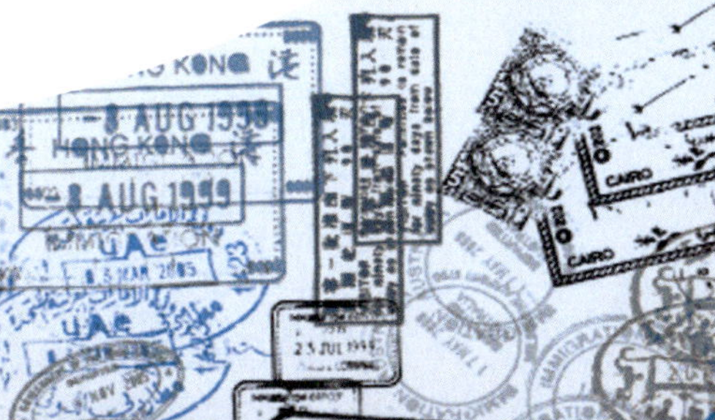

How did you get to France?

By plane / train / car / other ______

Date of arrival ______ Time ______ Date of departure______

All in all, we will stay in France for ______ days.

Is this your first visit ______ ?

Where will you sleep? hotel / campsite / apartment / with family / other ______

What sites are you planning on visiting?

____

____

____

What special activities are you planning on doing?

____

____

____

Are you excited about the trip?
This is an excitement indicator. Ask each family member how excited he or she is (from "not at all" up to "very, very much"), and mark it down on the indicator. Leonardo has also marked the level of his excitement…

not at all — very, very much

Leonardo

Who is traveling?

Write down the names of family members traveling with you.

Name:

Age:

Has he or she visited France before?
yes / no

What is the most exciting thing about your upcoming trip?

Name:

Age:

Has he or she visited France before?
yes / no

What is the most exciting thing about your upcoming trip?

Name:

Age:

Has he or she visited France before?
yes / no

What is the most exciting thing about your upcoming trip?

Name:

Age:

Has he or she visited France before?
yes / no

What is the most exciting thing about your upcoming trip?

Name:

Age:

Has he or she visited France before?
yes / no

What is the most exciting thing about your upcoming trip?

Name:

Age:

Has he or she visited France before?
yes / no

What is the most exciting thing about your upcoming trip?

Paste a picture of the whole family here.

Preparations at home – do not forget...!

Mom or Dad will take care of packing clothes (how many pairs of pants, which comb to take...). Leonardo will only suggest the stuff he thinks you should take along on your trip to France.

As you are going on vacation away from home, Leonardo recommends you take the following:

- *Kids' Travel Guide — France —* of course!
- comfortable walking shoes
- a raincoat (preferably folded — sometimes it rains without warning)
- a hat (and sunglasses, if you want)
- pens and pencils
- crayons and markers (It is always nice to color and draw.)
- a book
- your smart phone/tablet or camera

Pack a few things for the flight in a small bag (or backpack), such as:

- snacks, fruit, candy, and chewing gum. It may help a lot during takeoff and landing, when there's pressure in your ears.
- games you can play while sitting down: electronic games, booklets of crossword puzzles, connect-the-numbers (or connect-the-dots), etc.
- a notebook or a writing pad. You can use it for games, writing, or to draw or doodle in when you are bored...

Now let's see if you can find 12 items you should take on a trip in this word search puzzle:

P	A	T	I	E	N	C	E	A	W	F	G
E	L	R	T	S	G	Y	J	W	A	T	O
Q	E	Y	U	Y	K	Z	K	M	L	W	O
H	O	S	N	A	S	N	Y	S	K	G	D
A	N	R	Z	C	P	E	N	C	I	L	M
C	A	M	E	R	A	A	W	G	N	E	O
R	R	A	I	N	C	O	A	T	G	Q	O
Y	D	S	G	I	R	K	Z	K	S	H	D
S	O	A	C	O	A	E	T	K	H	A	T
F	R	U	I	T	Y	Q	O	V	O	D	A
B	O	O	K	F	O	H	Z	K	E	R	T
T	K	Z	K	A	N	S	I	E	S	Y	U
O	V	I	E	S	S	N	A	C	K	S	P

Leonardo, walking shoes, hat, raincoat, crayons, book, pencil, camera, snacks, fruit, patience, good mood

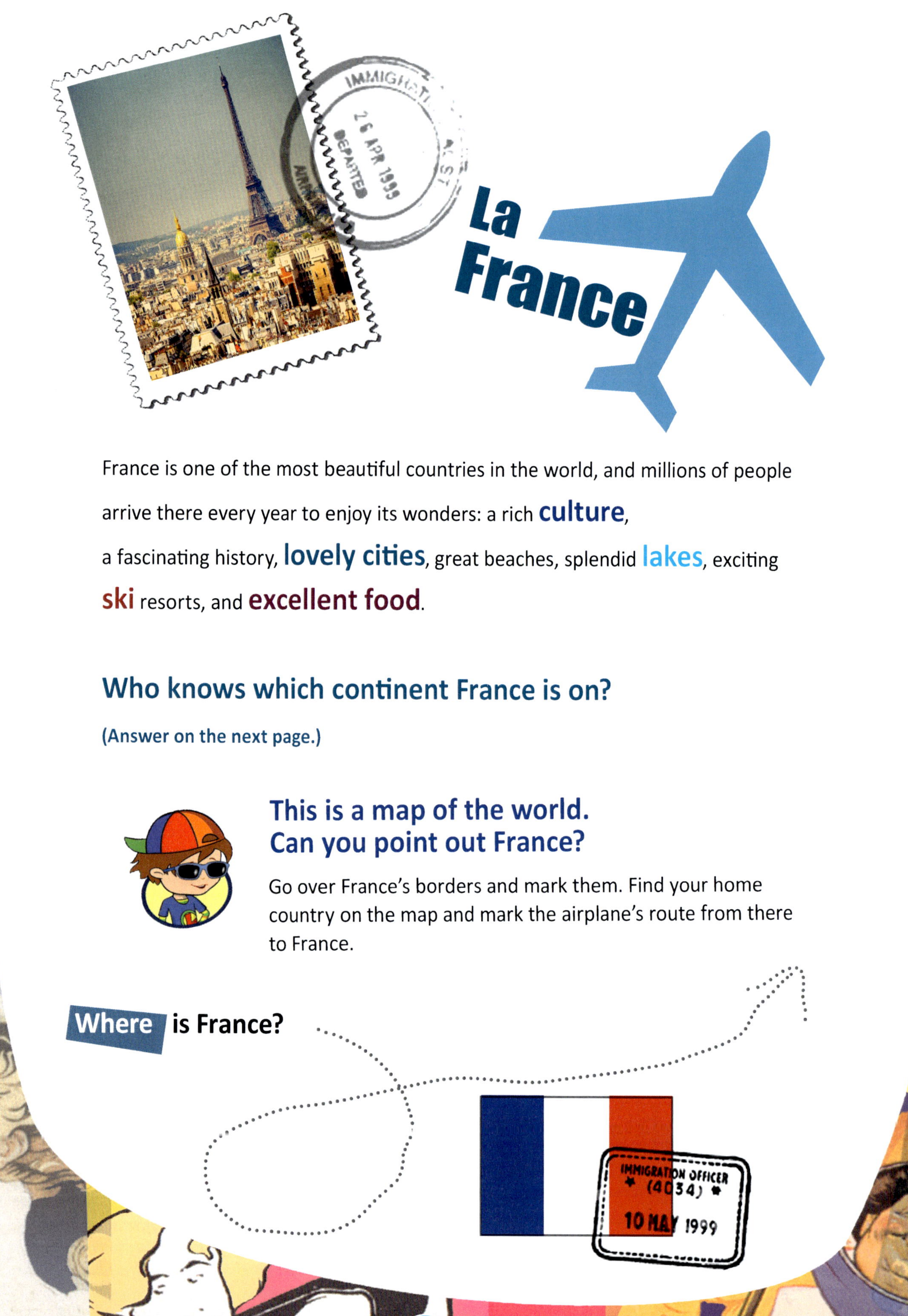

La France

France is one of the most beautiful countries in the world, and millions of people arrive there every year to enjoy its wonders: a rich **culture**, a fascinating history, **lovely cities**, great beaches, splendid **lakes**, exciting **ski** resorts, and **excellent food**.

Who knows which continent France is on?

(Answer on the next page.)

This is a map of the world. Can you point out France?

Go over France's borders and mark them. Find your home country on the map and mark the airplane's route from there to France.

Where is France?

France on the map

You may have noticed that France is located in the western part of Europe.
France is the third largest country in Europe. Only Russia and Ukraine are bigger.

What is a compass rose?

A compass rose is a drawing that shows the directions: North-South-East-West. North is always at the top of the map, and from that you can figure out the other directions.

When going on field trips, you can use a compass. A compass rose is drawn on the face of the compass, and the needle always points North.
Knowing each direction helps you navigate and find out where places are — or how to get from one point to another.

Mark the three missing directions in the blank squares.

North

France is surrounded by many neighboring countries. Can you find them on the map? If so, complete the following:

To the South — ________

To the East — ________, ________, and ________

To the North — ________ and ________

Answers: South — Spain; East — Italy, Switzerland, and Germany; North — Belgium and Luxembourg

Borders

Did you know?

In order to differentiate between countries, borders were invented. A border is a line that marks the end of one country's territory and the beginning of another. There are all kinds of borders; sometimes a river or a range of mountains are a natural border, or sometimes there is a fence or special gate to mark a border.
In France, for example, there's a natural border to the east: the French Alps, mountains that stretch between France, Italy, and Switzerland.

France is also surrounded by seas.
Can you find their names?
To the southeast ____________________

To the west ____________________

Quiz! What is the capital of France?

a. London

b. Elysees

c. Paris

d. The French Riviera

Answer: c. Paris

Answers: In the southeast: The Mediterranean;
In the West: The Atlantic Ocean

Do only French people live in France?

The majority of the people living in France are French (92 percent of its citizens), but there are also many immigrants* from North Africa and Germany.

*Immigrants are people who moved permanently to a country that is not their native country.

Do people in France speak French?

Of course! Most of the French people speak French, but if you listen carefully, you'll be able to hear other languages spoken as well. Most of these languages, such as Flemish, Alsatian, Breton, Basque, and Catalan, are not well-known.

Besides wonderful Paris, there are many other beautiful cities in France worth visiting.
Let's see if you can find 15 lovely French cities in the following word search puzzle.

A	S	C	H	E	R	B	O	U	R	G	H	I	K	Z
M	F	H	T	J	K	N	T	O	U	L	U	O	S	E
A	V	U	A	S	A	G	Z	N	Q	E	R	V	N	B
R	E	I	O	K	Z	T	O	A	I	L	H	E	L	E
S	L	P	R	R	J	R	E	N	M	C	J	I	I	H
E	G	B	L	I	L	L	E	T	Q	E	E	W	M	N
I	R	Y	E	M	G	K	L	E	E	Y	T	U	O	G
L	E	P	A	R	I	S	W	S	C	S	D	K	G	B
L	N	I	N	O	G	D	N	T	X	H	I	N	E	O
E	O	K	S	U	G	V	V	K	C	B	J	V	S	R
A	B	P	O	E	F	X	T	W	Q	A	O	Z	F	D
Q	L	Y	O	N	I	B	R	E	S	T	N	J	T	E
D	E	E	B	N	K	L	P	S	X	C	B	Y	T	A
D	T	M	O	N	T	E	C	A	R	L	O	G	E	U
J	I	R	F	G	H	K	O	C	A	M	U	J	M	X

Paris, Monte Carlo, Bordeaux, Orleans, Rouen, Toulouse, Nice, Marseille, Nantes, Lille, Cherbourg, Lyon, Dijon, Brest, Limoges, Grenoble

What other beautiful tourist attractions and sites are there in France?

The French Alps' beauty is overwhelming. The region is rich with high mountains, valleys, and sparkling **lakes** and **rivers**. Its beauty attracts many tourists from all over the world. In winter, you can go **skiing** on the snowy mountain slopes, and in summer **enjoy the scenic drives in nature.**

What is a valley? A lowland surrounded by mountains or hills.

The French Riviera is a resort area, famous in France and worldwide. In French, the Riviera is called *La Côte D'Azure*, meaning "sky-blue coast." There are small resort villages in the Riviera, beautiful cities such as Marseille, Cannes, and Monaco, and naturally, some splendid and exotic beaches. It is said that the residents of this region are not at all like the typical French people; they are much more relaxed and calm (no wonder... 😉). The rich and the famous love to spend time in the French Riviera, and you may be lucky enough to see a famous movie star driving by in a fancy car...

Flags, symbols, and coins

This is the **flag** of **France**.

The French call it *Le Tricolore*. If you don't know what 'tricolor" means, take a look at the flag and try to figure it out by counting the number of colors ("tri" means three) 😉.

Did you know?

In the past, each stripe was of a different width. It was Napoleon who decided that the stripes should all be the same size, and he changed the flag — although the French army still uses the old one.

This is the symbol of France. If you take a close look, you can see that there are two kinds of leaves: olive leaves, which symbolize peace, and oak leaves, which stand for eternity (because the oak is a very strong tree). The axe is justice, while the letters RF are the first initials of the words "French Republic," or as the French say: *La Republique Francaise.*

If you want to buy something in France, how do you pay for it?

Up until a few years ago, the French had their own currency, the franc. In 1999, the **franc** was replaced by the European currency named the **euro**.

The French Alps

The European Union (EU)

The European Union is a federation of 27 countries in Europe. Each is independent, but they all have some common characteristics, like their currency (money). If you visit Spain, Germany, or France, you will use the euro, even though each of these countries is independent and stands on its own.

This is the French franc.

And this is the euro.

Did you know?

If the European Union were one big country (like the United States of America, which is made up of 50 states), it would be the third largest country in the world.

The flag of the European Union

If you want to buy a souvenir in France, what currency will you use?

Answer: Euro, of course!

Once, many years ago...

Have you ever heard of the French Revolution? Or maybe the name Napoleon rings a bell? 😉 The history of France is fascinating.

People have lived in the area that is now called France as far back as the Stone Age. Back then it was not called "France," of course. As in all countries that have been in existence for many years, France was ruled throughout the ages by kings, **tyrants,*** and sovereigns. But for over 130 years now, France has been headed by presidents. Let us try to put things in order so that we can understand France's history.

*A tyrant is an evil ruler.

In ancient times, the area where France is now was called **Gaul**, and it was inhabited by the Gallic tribes. Julius Caesar conquered Gaul and added it to the Roman Empire. In the sixth century, more than 1,400 years ago, Gaul was overrun by Germanic tribes called the "Franks." They were led by King Karl the Great, who conquered France as well as large areas of **Europe**. Although it was a powerful, vast empire, it did not last long. During the reign of **Karl the Great's** grandchildren, the empire was divided, and its **western part** became a separate kingdom, known today as **France.**

Through the years, many kings ruled the kingdom, but around 1000 AD, one dynasty* of kings came to power and ruled France for 800 years.

Karl the Great

*Dynasty: a succession of rulers from the same family. The king's son is the heir to the king, and he becomes the king next. Then his son replaces him, and so on. Thus the kingship remains in the family.

Did you know?

One of the most famous wars that took place during these years was the **Hundred Years' War** between France and England. You are probably guessing that it lasted 100 years... The truth is, it lasted 116 years (from 1337 until 1453)!

Louis the 14th was a famous king who ruled France from 1661 until 1715. He was the most powerful and well-known king of all European monarchs, and you will read more about him later.

Have you ever heard about the French Revolution?

About 70 years after the reign of Louis the 14th, France was going through a difficult period. The kings who ruled the country were evil and dishonest. They imposed high taxes on the people, didn't care about their hardships, and prevented them from getting an education. The kings seized people's lands, wasted money, and plunged France into a tough economic situation.

The situation became unbearable until the people united — the peasants, the educated people, and the workers — and fought against the rule of the kings. A war broke out in 1789, and that is what we call the **French Revolution**. It is an important event in the history of France and the world, because the common people succeeded in revolting and putting an end to the kingship. The kingdom was replaced by a republic — a form of government by the people.

King Louis the 14th

Did you know?

Many people in France were so poor that they could not even buy bread to eat, but the royalty did not care. It is said that the royal family was so removed from the common people that when Queen Marie-Antoinette heard that the people had no bread, she responded, "Let them eat cake!"

The republic did not last long, and after a short period of chaos, **Napoleon Bonaparte** came to power and declared himself Emperor (you will learn about him later).

In 1814, France and Germany became bitter enemies and began to fight each other constantly. In 1914, the First World War broke out, and France joined the Allies who fought the Germans. Many French soldiers were killed, but thanks to the assistance of the **American army**, Germany was defeated.

The war cost much money, and France's economy fell into difficulty. The French people were hungry again.

During World War II, which broke out in 1939, France once again fought **Germany**, but the strong German army defeated the French and conquered large parts of France. The Germans took over much of France for about five years — until 1944 — when the Allied Forces* landed in Normandy in northern France. They freed the areas under German control, and **France was once again reunited**.

***The "Allied Forces" were a military force made up of soldiers from several countries who fought together against Germany.**

At the end of the war, France invested heavily in creating work and financial stability and was slowly rehabilitated.

This is how soliders once looked.

Famous leaders and rulers

Let us meet a few of the leaders and rulers who influenced France throughout the years:

Pleased to meet you — King Louis the 14th

King Louis the 14th lived from 1638 to 1715 and was one of the strongest monarchs in the history of France. He used to say, **"I am the state,"** because he thought he was the most **important** person in France — and the only one who had the authority to make decisions.

The father of Louis the 14th (King Louis the 13th, of course), died prematurely, and young Prince Louis was crowned King at the age of five! His mother, Queen Anne, replaced him until he grew up and was old enough to sit on the throne.

Louis the 14th was a very **smart king**. He built his palace in Versailles (and not in the capital, Paris), and by doing so, he succeeded in removing those who tried to weaken him and take over the kingship. He spent the first part of his reign **fighting** his neighbors — Holland, Belgium, and Germany. A succession of impressive **victories** helped him strengthen and establish France as a leading country in Europe. But the final years of his reign were difficult and unpleasant for the French people. King Louis conquered Spain, but the cost of the war was high and its **large expenses** led France to an **economic crisis.**

Nevertheless, in the history of France, King Louis the 14th is regarded as a prominent and powerful monarch.

Among his impressive achievements are the building of the **Palace of Versailles** — which is considered the finest example of architecture and art in France — and the design of gardens and furniture that still bear his name: "Louis the 14th" style.

King Louis the 14th

Pleased to meet you — Napoleon Bonaparte

Napoleon Bonaparte was France's most significant ruler in the 19th century, and his influence spread all over Europe.

Did you know?

It is thought that Napoleon was a short man, but this is not true. The mistake is a result of the difference between the French measurement system and the English one. At his death, Napoleon was slightly taller than 5 French feet. The French "foot" was longer than the English one, so Napoleon was actually about 1.68 meters (or about 5 feet, 6 inches) tall, which was not considered so short in his time.

Napoleon was a brilliant military commander, known all over Europe for his great victories and many conquests. He was only **24 years old** when he was appointed general and commanded the French army. He was famous for his ability to build a **war strategy** that led to victories nobody thought were possible.

At the age of 35, Napoleon became the **ruler of France** after the turbulent times of the French Revolution. He succeeded in stabilizing the country and taking care of its citizens. A year and a half after being made the Emperor of the French, he was also crowned King of Italy.

Did you know?

During that period, the Pope crowned the emperors, to symbolize that the emperor was subject to the Church and the Pope. During Napoleon's coronation as Emperor of the French, however, he took the crown from the Pope and placed it on his own head — as if to say that he, Napoleon, did not wish to be lesser than anyone!

Napoleon Bonaparte

Napoleon married **Josephine de Beauharnais**, but they were divorced 13 years later. (It is said the reason was that Josephine couldn't have children.) Napoleon then married **Marie-Louise of Austria**, daughter of the Emperor of Austria, possibly in order to unite the two nations.

Despite his impressive achievements, Napoleon's end was tragic. His army suffered a great loss in a war against Russia. Out of 500,000 soldiers who went to war, less than 100,000 survived, and Napoleon returned to Paris **defeated** and **humiliated**. Napoleon's position became unstable, and a group of allied countries united in order to defeat the French army. They **conquered** Paris, forced Napoleon to leave his office, and sent him away to exile on the isle of Elba.

A short while later, Napoleon tried to recruit an army of volunteers in order to fight and get back his position as emperor. The famous Battle of **Waterloo** was Napoleon's last battle, and he was beaten by the English army. He was driven away from France and exiled to the island of St. Helena, where he spent the rest of his life. **Napoleon died before his 52nd birthday.**

Napoleon left an impressive legacy: imposing **architectural structures** (such as the Arch of Triumph — which you will read about later), and a code of advanced laws that did not exist until his time. These included the **Equality Laws,** which state that all human beings are born equal and all have a right to acquire property.

Napoleon is also remembered for his brilliant quotes.* Here are some of them:

"An army marches on its stomach."

"You are longer than me, not taller." (This was his answer to a soldier who claimed to be taller than Napoleon.)

"If you want a thing done well, do it yourself."

"You can do everything with a spear, except sit on it."

*"Quote" means to repeat words or sentences that someone else said.

Pleased to meet you — Charles de Gaulle

Charles de Gaulle was **one of the greatest politicians of the 20th century**. He was born in 1890 and died 80 years later. De Gaulle was a young and gifted officer. He was known for his ability to thwart German military tactics during **World War II, when Germany** was trying to invade France and other parts of Europe. Following the German invasion of France, de Gaulle escaped to England and was appointed Prime Minister in Exile (a prime minister who runs his country from another place). In 1944, de Gaulle entered Paris at the head of the **Allied Forces,** liberated the city from the Germans, and became famous all over the world.

In the late 1940s, de Gaulle opposed the way France was run and retired from military and political life. However, in 1958 he was called back to **head the country** when times were difficult economically and politically. During his period as **president**, de Gaulle strengthened France's economy and its position in the world, and made France a powerful, independent country.

Did you know?
About 75 million visitors go to France annually, much more than the number of tourists who visit Spain or the United States, for example.

Who am I?

Quizzes!

- Although I was considered a short man, I am the most famous military figure in the history of France.
- Despite the fact that France suffered economic hardships during my time, I am regarded as its most successful king.
- Thanks to me, France today is a modern and powerful state.

Answers: (1) Napoleon; (2) Louis the 14th; (3) De Gaulle

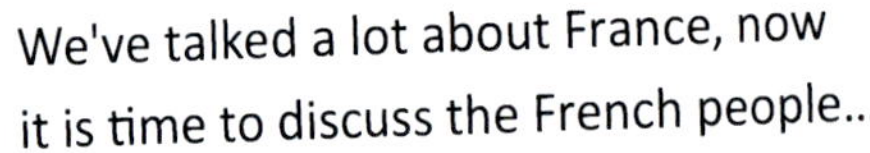
We've talked a lot about France, now
it is time to discuss the French people...

Culture and customs

Do you know any French people? **Have you ever heard the names Jean-Paul, Pierre, Jacques, or Marie-Louise?** We've talked a lot about France, but what about the French people?

What is unique about the French? What do they like to do in their **spare time?** Where do they work? Which **customs are unique** to France?

- The French appreciate food and like to talk about it. They not only enjoy cooking and buying good food, but they also arrange the food on the plate in a special, fine way (a chapter will be dedicated to French food).

- The French are aesthetic people. Their well-planned streets and avenues, their lovely gardens, their excellent taste in fashion, and their food markets — which sometimes look like food museums — make it is easy to understand the French admiration for beauty and aesthetics.*

*Aesthetics: a branch of philosophy dealing with the criticism of art, the nature of beauty, and the awareness of it.

- Their patriotism: You may have noticed that the French love their culture, especially their language. It seems as if they don't even make an effort to speak or understand other languages. Most of the signs, the menus in the restaurants, and the tourism booklets are written in French only. Even foreign TV programs — and not only those for children — are dubbed* into French!

*Dub: to record voices over the actors' voices in a film put the film's dialogue in a different language.

What impression did the French make on you?

1. They are charming.
2. They are quite nice.
3. Not so nice...
4. I cannot make up my mind.

Bon appétit! — French cuisine (cooking)

The French are known for their **excellent, tasty dishes.** Most adults will tell you that the French style of cooking is superb (they may use other descriptions, but they all agree that the cuisine is excellent 😉).

The French love to eat. They may not eat large quantities of food, but they love to **buy** it, **prepare** it, and **talk** about it.

You cannot go to France without knowing certain basic and important facts about French food. Leonardo will give you some idea about what is going on:

Where to eat

A patisserie

— a bakery with sweet cakes and pastries. The shop windows of the patisseries are so beautiful and yummy that you may want to take their picture. Why not?

Paste a souvenir picture of a patisserie's shop window here.

Cremerie — a store for cheese

- **Boulangerie** — a shop for bread and cakes. Some of these shops bake their own pastries in a bakery at the back of the store, and the smell that comes from them is wonderful.
- **Cremerie** — a store for cheese. For those of you who like cheese, this is heaven...
- **Café** — when you say "café" in French, it means a coffee shop. Most cafés serve light lunches as well.
- **Brasserie** — a large restaurant serving local food and alcoholic beverages.
- **Bistro** — a small restaurant serving simple meals in a homey setting.
- **Food markets** — there are several food markets in France and visiting them is a wonderful experience — the smells, the colors, and the variety of groceries are delightful.

Now that we've learned about the places where you can eat, let's get to know some of the tasty dishes you should eat when in France. When you sit in a restaurant and look at the menu, or stand in line at a patisserie, take a look at the list below and find these recommended dishes:

Pastries

If you don't like to try new foods (meat or side dishes), ask your parents to order a tasty sandwich. Paris is a paradise for bread lovers. If you like anything made of dough and baked in an oven, then try these: brioche (a kind of light-textured bread), an éclair (pastry filled with cream and covered in chocolate), or a croissant, of course.

Cheese

France is famous for its variety of cheese. It is recommended to taste Camembert, Pont l'Éyvêque and chevre (goat cheese). The French sour cream, called "crème fraiche," is very tasty.

Meat

If you wish to order chicken, look for the word *poulet* in the menu. If you want veal, look for *veau*.

And what about desserts?

The names of traditional French desserts are enough to make your mouth water:

- Tart Tatin (an upside-down apple pie)
- Profiterole (a small, round cream puff served with ice cream and hot chocolate sauce)
- Flan (baked custard — a sort of pudding)
- Crème Brulee (custard topped with a layer of hard caramel)

And how can we do without... a chocolate mousse!

Pastries

Leonardo has just landed in France, and he already has the urge to try some delicious foods. Help him find them...

Where can he find some good cheese? ____________

Where can he find tasty bread? ____________

And if he wants something sweet to eat, where would you advise him to go? ____________

Answers: A cremerie; A boulangerie; A patisserie

What new dishes did you see?
More importantly, what new dishes did you taste?

Name of the dish (if you don't know its name, write down what it looks like)	Did you taste it? (yes or no)	Description of dish (what does it include; how does it look)	How do you grade it? (bad, good, or excellent)

Did you taste a dish that looks exactly like something you eat at home, but tastes different?

____

____

Majority rules! A family vote:

Which dish was voted as favorite among your family members?

Name	What dish did you like the best?

The winning dish is: ____________________

How do you say it in French...?
(a handy dictionary)

It is easy to recognize the French language. When you hear it, you know right away what it is. Some French words sound almost the same in English (for example, "dinner" in English and *le dinner* in French) because both languages were derived from Latin.

Do you want to feel a little independent and speak some French?

Here are some words that will help you. You can practice them later on...

Being polite

Hello/good morning	Bonjour
Good evening	Bonsoir
Bye-bye/see you	Au revoir
Yes	Oui
No	Non
Please	S'il vous plait
Thank you	Merci
Thank you very much	Merci beaucoup
You're welcome	De rien
Excuse me	Excusez moi
Sorry/pardon me	Pardon
I do not speak French.	Je ne parle pas Francais.
Do you speak English?	Parlez vous Anglais?

At the restaurant

Restaurant	Restaurant
Breakfast	Le petit dejeuner
Lunch	Le dejeuner
Dinner	Le dinner
Butter	Du beurre
Bread	Du pain
A cup	Une tasse
A glass	Un verre
Fork	Une fourchette
Knife	Un couteau
Spoon	Une cuillere
Sugar	Du sucre
Wine	Du vin
Salt	Du sel
Pepper	Du poivre
Croissants	Des croissants
Honey	Du miel
Eggs	Des oeufs
An omelette	Une omelette
Snails	Des escargots
Sausage	Du saucisson
Salad	Une salade
Soup	Une soup
Fish	Du poisson
Meat	La viande
Beef	Le boeuf
Lamb	Le mouton
Pork	Le pork
Steak	Le steak
Veal	Le veau
Chicken	Le poulet
Noodles	Les nouilles
Pasta	Les pates
Potatoes	Les pommes de terre
Cheese	Du fromage
The bill	La note

Competition!

Who remembers more French words?

Ask each other and award points for each correctly remembered word.

Who won?

Need to buy something?

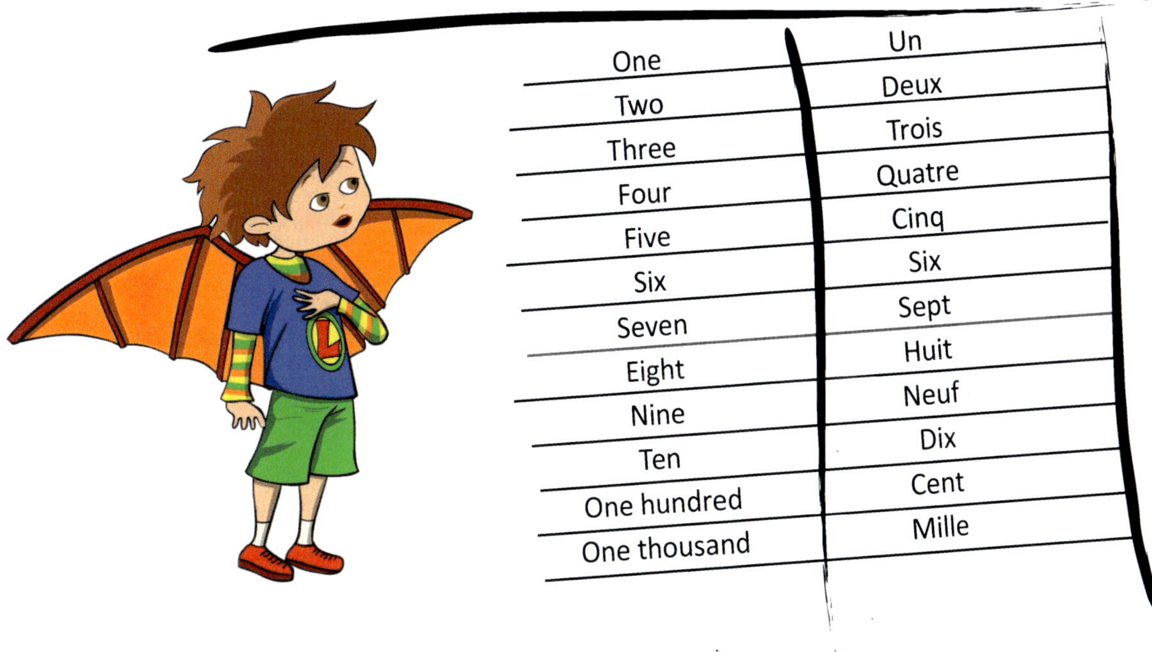

One	Un
Two	Deux
Three	Trois
Four	Quatre
Five	Cinq
Six	Six
Seven	Sept
Eight	Huit
Nine	Neuf
Ten	Dix
One hundred	Cent
One thousand	Mille

Practice a few sentences to help you memorize the words:

- In English — Excuse me, I don't speak French.

  In French — Excusez moi je ne parle pas Francais.

- In English — How much is a ticket to the subway (the Metro)?

  In French — ________________

- In English — Good evening, where is the train station?

  In French — ________________

- Say your home phone number in French.
- Count from 1 to 10 in French.
- Say your hotel room number in French.

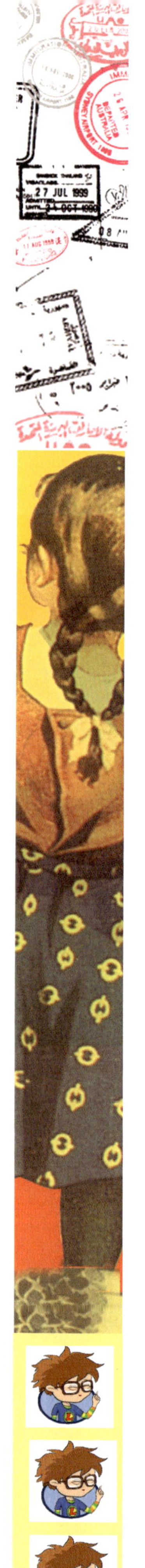

And to sum it all up...

Summary of the trip

We had great fun — what a pity it is over...

Which places in France did you visit?

____

Whom did you meet...

- Did you meet tourists from other countries? Yes / No

  If you did meet tourists, where did they come from?

  (Name their nationalities):

____

____

Shopping and souvenirs...

- What did you buy on the trip?

____

____

- What did you want to buy, but ended up not buying?

____

____

Grade the most beautiful places and the best experiences of your journey:

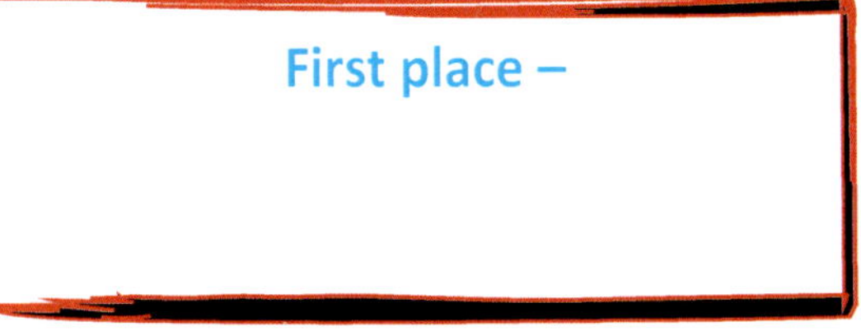

First place –

Second place –

Third place –

And now, a difficult task — discuss it with your family and decide...

What did you enjoy most on the trip?

Games and activities

Take turns and have each family member insert the words in one or two of the sentences. A funny story will come out!

Yesterday morning we drove to ________. We met ______ and ______.
We suggested they join us. They said _____________ and went to _____.
When we neared ____, we saw the ________. We were really surprised.
At first, we thought it was ______, but pretty soon we realized that it was ________. ______ said that the best thing would be to ________ and we all agreed.
When we reached the hotel, we decided to _________. Most of us thought it was a bad idea, but in the end, we all agreed. When we started walking towards _________, we found out ______________.
That is why we have decided to drop the whole thing. We went back to __________ pretty tired but happy.

Solve the mystery of the three tourists...

Use the clues to figure out where the tourists are from, what they're wearing, and what they are doing on their vacation. Write the answers in the table:

- The three tourists arrived from Israel, America, and England.
- The tourist wearing the suit drinks tea.
- The tourist who drinks tea is not from America or Israel.
- The tourist with the pants and shirt didn't drink tea and didn't take any pictures today.
- The tourist from America is resting on the bench.
- The tourist who is taking pictures arrived on a night flight from Israel.
- The tourist from England is not wearing jeans and is not resting on the bench.

	What does he wear?	Where is he from?	What is he doing?
Tourist A			
Tourist B			
Tourist C			

Answers on page 37.

The words got lost...

Sort the words according to their numbers. Each set of numbers makes a sentence. Find the sentences and write them below:

4 the	2 France	7 the	1 what	8 Versailles	3 Paris	8 Palace	4 arch	5 Notre	1 fun	5 Dame
3 is	5 is	8 was	5 one	8 built	6 one	7 obelisk	8 by	2 is	8 king	7 is
6 of	1 we	4 of	2 located	6 the	7 the	5 of	4 triumph	3 also	8 Louis	5 the
5 most	3 called	8 the	5 famous	6 world's	4 commem-orates	3 the	8 14th	7 symbol	1 are	7 of
1 going	4 Napoleon's	2 in	6 biggest	3 city	7 the	4 army's	6 museums	5 cathedrals	3 of	1 to
2 Europe	5 in	6 is	7 Concorde	6 the	4 victory	7 Square	5 Europe	1 Paris	6 Louvre	3 light

1. ______

2. ______

3. ______

4. ______

5. ______

6. ______

7. ______

8. ______

Answers on page 37.

Trivia

1. On what continent is France located?
2. True or false? France is the third largest country in Europe.
3. Which natural border separates France, Italy, and Switzerland?
4. True or false? The French Alps is the name of a river.
5. What is the French flag called?

6. What colors appear on the French flag?
7. What currency is used in France?
8. True or false? The Arch of Triumph was built by King Louis the 14th.
9. Complete: “If they don’t have bread, let them eat...”
10. True or false? Napoleon met his death while fighting in a battle for the glory of France.
11. Which famous French king was crowned at the age of five?
12. True or false? Charles de Gaulle was the king who built the Versailles Palace.
13. Who built the Versailles Palace?
14. What is a patisserie?
15. How do you pronounce "croissant"?
16. What is Tart Tatin?
17. How do you say ”Good morning” in French?

Answers on page 37.

Trivia (page 36)

Answers

1. Europe
2. True (after Russia and Ukraine)
3. The French Alps
4. False (It's the name of a mountain range that separates France, Italy, and Switzerland.)
5. The Tricolor (for the three colors that appear on it)
6. Blue, white, and red
7. The euro
8. False (The Arch of Triumph was built by Napoleon to commemorate his big victories in battle.)
9. Cake (said by Queen Marie-Antoinette)
10. False (He died on the island of St. Helena after he lost the Battle of Waterloo and was exiled from France.)
11. King Louis the 14th
12. False (Charles de Gaulle was one of the strong people who helped to rebuild France and turn it into a great power.)
13. King Loius the 14th
14. A pastry bakery
15. Krwas-son
16. A famous French dessert — sort of an upside-down apple pie
17. Bonjour

Words got lost (page 35)

1. What fun — we are going to Paris.
2. France is located in Europe.
3. Paris is also called the City of Light.
4. The Arch of Triumph commemorates Napoleon's army's victory.
5. Notre-Dame is one of the most famous cathedrals in Europe.
6. One of the biggest museums in the world is the Louvre.
7. The obelisk is the symbol of the Concorde Square.
8. Versailles Palace was built by King Louis the 14th.

Solve the mystery of the three tourists (page 34)

	What does he wear?	Where is he from?	What is he doing?
Tourist A	Jeans	Israel	Taking pictures
Tourist B	Pants and a shirt	America	Resting on the bench
Tourist C	A suit	England	Drinking tea

Coloring page

L'Arc de Triomphe (the Arch of Triumph)

Date	What did we do?

Date	What did we do?

Made in the USA
Lexington, KY
21 January 2019